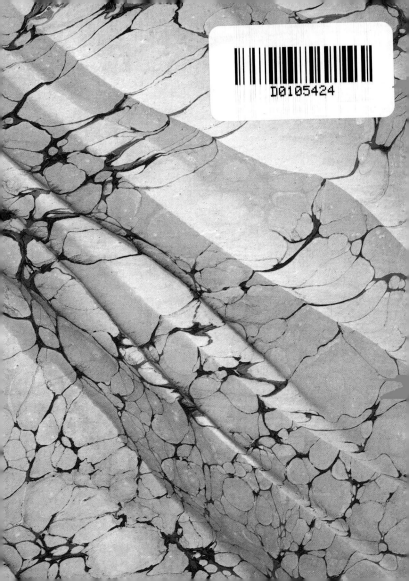

THE BANTAM LIBRARY
of Culinary Arts

NUTS

JILL NORMAN

BANTAM BOOKS

TORONTO · NEW YORK · LONDON · SYDNEY · AUCKLAND

A DORLING KINDERSLEY BOOK

NUTS

A BANTAM BOOK/PUBLISHED BY ARRANGEMENT WITH
DORLING KINDERSLEY LIMITED

PRINTING HISTORY
DORLING KINDERSLEY EDITION
PUBLISHED IN GREAT BRITAIN IN 1990

BANTAM EDITION/MAY 1991

EDITOR LAURA HARPER
SENIOR EDITOR CAROLYN RYDEN
AMERICAN EDITOR BECKY CABAZA
DESIGN MATHEWSON BULL
PHOTOGRAPHER DAVE KING

Every effort has been made to provide accurate conversions from metric to American measures,
though some ingredient amounts have been rounded off to the closest American measure.

LIBRARY OF CONGRESS CATALOGING-IN-PUBLICATION DATA

NORMAN, JILL.
NUTS/JILL NORMAN.
P. CM. – (THE BANTAM LIBRARY OF CULINARY ARTS)
INCLUDES INDEX.
1. COOKERY (NUTS) 2. NUTS.
I. TITLE. II. SERIES.
TX814.N67 1991
641.6'45–DC20
90-40242   CIP
ISBN 0-553-07219-6

PRINTED AND BOUND IN HONG KONG BY IMAGO
0 9 8 7 6 5 4 3 2 1

CONTENTS

INTRODUCTION

*I*N THE WEST *we consume large quantities of nuts, usually roasted and salted, while having a drink, or as a snack between meals. Green almonds and fresh walnuts may still be offered with a glass of sweet wine at the end of a leisurely meal – a practice that goes back to antiquity.*

We have never regarded nuts as a serious part of our diet, although we are now more conscious of their protein, fat, and mineral content. However, in other parts of the world nuts are an essential element in the diet, often used to supplement vegetable protein when meat or fish is not available or too expensive.

From West Africa across to Ethiopia, peanuts predominate. Roasted and ground, they are a constant ingredient in soups and stews. In Malay and Indonesian cooking a rich peanut sauce accompanies satay (small skewers of grilled meat).

In southern India cashews and coconut come into their own. Fried or toasted cashews are considered a delicacy when added to vegetable dishes, while all parts of the coconut make a contribution to the economy. In the north almonds and pistachios, two nuts once much favored by the Mogul emperors, are still widely used. Slivered or ground, toasted or plain, they are found in pilafs, in delicately spiced savory dishes of chicken or meat, and in puddings.

The Persians and Arabs use ground nuts – almonds, hazelnuts, walnuts, or pistachios – to add body and flavor to long-cooked meat dishes, and to make rich sauces for poultry. The Arabs and Turks are masters of varied pastries filled with chopped nuts, and drenched in honey. Pine nuts, the delicately flavored seeds of the Mediterranean stone pine, are added to rice dishes, stuffings, jams, and sweetmeats.

Farther west, around the Mediterranean, pine nuts are still more common; all the regions of Italy have specialties using pine nuts – with marinated sardines in Venice, spinach in Rome, swordfish in Sicily, and to make pesto in Genoa. In Spain every small grocer sells pine nuts and they are cooked with rabbit, or chicken, added to sauces for fish, or made into sweetmeats. In northern Europe almonds, hazelnuts and walnuts are the main nuts used in baking. Chestnuts can be bought roasted on street corners in autumn, but they also make excellent desserts and vegetable dishes.

French chestnut purée label, c. 1930

North America is the home of the pecan, once described as "a walnut in a torpedo," a good nut for desserts and confectionery. Other nuts are cultivated widely in the United States, particularly almonds, walnuts, pistachios, and peanuts.

Nuts are certainly one of our most versatile foods and in Western cooking their possibilities are often underrated. The recipes in this little book come from all parts of the world to tempt you to increase your repertoire of dishes in which nuts can be used.

ALMOND

*T*HE ALMONDS WE EAT *are the fruit of* Prunus amygdalus *(var.* dulcis*) which probably originated in the Near East but has long been grown throughout the Mediterranean region, including North Africa, and in other warm (but not tropical) zones from Kashmir to California and southern Australia. The Moguls adored them, so did the Romans. Their universal popularity has made them the dominant nuts in world trade, with Italy, Spain, and California being the main exporters.*

Whole almonds

Almonds in their skin　　　*Blanched and peeled almonds*

Almonds are the most important nuts in gastronomy. Many go into baking and confectionery (from tarts to marzipan). Oriental countries use them with rice (pilafs or stuffings), with poultry or meat – the West with fish. Ground almonds flavor and thicken soups and sauces. Almonds are added to salads and savory dips. Real almond essence is made from bitter almonds (var. *amara*), which also flavor ratafias and macaroons.

Almond flakes

Sugared almonds

Coarse ground almonds

HAZELNUT

*M*ANY SPECIES *of hazelnut grow wild in temperate Asia, Europe, and America, but only three are cultivated:* Coryllus avellana, *the cobnut of the Old World's temperate zones,* C. maxima, *the filbert of the Mediterranean region, overlapping in the Middle East with* C. colurna, *the Turkish hazel. Filberts have husks that extend well beyond the nut, cobs do not – but once they are shelled they are hard to tell apart, except that the Turkish hazel is smaller than the others. North America now cultivates only the* avellana *species.*

Hazelnuts have long been used as a raw food, gathered in the wild since Mesolithic times, and found in the stores of Bronze Age settlements. Now the most important exporters are Italy, Spain, Turkey, France, and northwest Africa. Other countries grow them for home consumption only.

Hazelnut oil

Filberts

Hazelnuts

Most nuts are eaten fresh, used in cakes and confections such as the various *tortone* (Italian nougats), or made into *gianduia* paste for fillings. Very young, fresh hazelnuts are good in salads – so is hazelnut oil.

Only Spain has created an extensive and inventive cuisine based on the hazelnut, culminating in the many versions of *salsa romesco*.

WALNUT

*T*HE WALNUT, Juglans regia, native to the temperate zone of Europe and Asia, has long been introduced to similar climates all over the world. Ancient Greece and Rome held it in esteem for its timber as well as its fruit, but the tree did not reach Britain until the 15th century. France, where walnuts are known just as nuts, is the main producer, closely followed by California and Oregon, Italy and Romania. China's large crop is used entirely in the home market.

Walnuts

Green
walnuts

The large American black
walnut, *J. nigra*, hard to crack
and not as good to eat as the European
varieties, is used mainly for flavoring,
while the white walnut or butternut, *J. cinerea*,
finds its way into confectionery. The unripe
green fruit can be made into pickles or preserved in
syrup. John Evelyn praised its use as a salad.
Fresh "wet" walnuts are a delicacy. Fully ripe nuts are eaten as
dessert ("across the walnuts and the wine" – Tennyson) and used
in baking and confectionery. Walnut oil makes fine dressings for
salads and pasta and also goes into artists' paint.

BRAZIL NUT

*B*RAZIL NUTS, *as the name suggests, originated in South America. The giant* Bertholettia excelsa *tree grows in the tropical forests of the Amazon region and produces fruit as large as a man's head, weighing several pounds and holding up to two dozen of the hard three-sided nuts, clustered together like segments of an orange. Although sporadically grown elsewhere, most nuts are still gathered in the wild in both Brazil and Venezuela.*

The Brazil nut, and even more so its close relation the sapucaya (*Lecythus zabucajo*), is underrated and little used – perhaps because it is hard to crack and, once cracked, goes rancid quickly since it is 65 percent oil. The nuts often substitute well for almonds and are very easy to grate or grind.

Shelled Brazil nuts

Brazil nuts

CASHEW

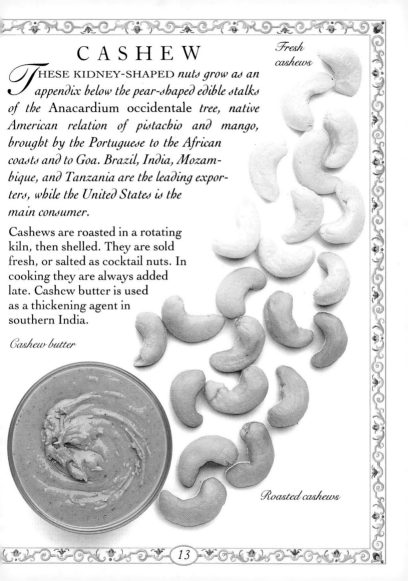

*T*HESE KIDNEY-SHAPED *nuts grow as an appendix below the pear-shaped edible stalks of the* Anacardium occidentale *tree, native American relation of pistachio and mango, brought by the Portuguese to the African coasts and to Goa. Brazil, India, Mozambique, and Tanzania are the leading exporters, while the United States is the main consumer.*

Cashews are roasted in a rotating kiln, then shelled. They are sold fresh, or salted as cocktail nuts. In cooking they are always added late. Cashew butter is used as a thickening agent in southern India.

Fresh cashews

Cashew butter

Roasted cashews

PEANUT

THE PEA that poses as a nut, Arachis hypogaea *of the* Legu-minosae *family, stems from South America, but wherever it occurs these days (and that is in almost every subtropical region) it was planted by man. The Portuguese took it to West Africa, from where much later it was taken to North America, to Goa, from where it spread through India, and to the East Indies. China and India are the main pro-ducers now, but their entire crop is used at home – the rest of the world imports peanuts mostly from West Africa, es-pecially Nigeria.*

Peanuts

Shelled peanuts

Peanuts are important ingredients in West African cooking, especially as a roasted meal used to thicken soups and stews. In Malaysia and Indonesia peanut paste forms the base for *satay* sauces and for a dressing for vegetables called *gado gado*.

Crunchy peanut butter

Salted peanuts

In the Western world peanuts have many uses. Roasted, they are salted as cocktail snacks or ground into peanut butter – used on its own or for cooking. Many confections with peanuts are popular (peanut brittle, sugar- or chocolate-coated peanuts). The oil can be used for cooking and on salads.

Peanut oil

COCONUT

*T*HE TALL Cocos nucifera *palm grows on every tropical shore, but its place of origin is obscure. It fruits throughout the year, making it a steady supplier of many necessities: fiber from the husk for rope and mats, the half shells as utensils, the flesh eaten fresh or dried. The dried flesh, known as copra, yields an oil much used for cosmetics and margarine. The Philippines and Indonesia are its main exporters, but many small Pacific islands depend on coconuts too.*

Coconut milk, pressed from the flesh soaked in water, is essential to the cuisine of Indonesia and Malaysia as the main thickening agent. It is also used in West Africa and on the "slave coasts" of Colombia and Brazil to cook a rich and flavorful rice, and in India for sauces called *molee*. Dry shredded coconut is the main form used in Western baking.

It can be soaked to make coconut milk but coconut cream is better and easier.

Coconut cream

Coconut

Grated fresh
coconut

Dried
coconut

CHESTNUT

*T*HE SWEET CHESTNUT, Castanea sativa, *is a native of southern Europe that has long become popular in other temperate zones for its timber as well as its nuts. The Romans may have brought the tree to Britain, much as early settlers took it to North America, where the native* C. dentata *has perished in a blight. The Japanese* C. crenata *and several other varieties are also edible.*

Chestnuts

Shelled chestnuts

Chestnuts are the only nuts to be treated as a vegetable: they contain much starch and little oil. Ground, they make good flour, but not for bread: the flour lacks gluten.

Peeled chestnuts

Both the husk and the brown skin of the nut must be taken off before the nuts are ready for further use.

Marrons glacés

Boiled or roasted, ground or puréed or whole, chestnuts go into soups, stews, stuffings, and desserts. *Marrons glacés* are chestnuts poached in syrup.

Whole chestnuts

Chestnut purée

PINE NUT

*T*HE NUTS *of many pine trees are sought-after delicacies in countries as far apart as northern India* (chilgoza), *Chile (the monkey puzzle), and the American southwest, where Indians still gather the* piñons *of the two-leaved pine. Only* Pinus pinea, *the stone pine, which grows wild from Portugal to the Black Sea, is cultivated for commerce.*

In the Middle East, pine nuts go into sweetmeats, stuffings, and pilafs. Italy and Spain prefer them with vegetables and as a thickening for sauces such as *pesto* (from Genoa, which has an inventive pine nut cuisine). Also popular are chocolate-coated nuts and American *piñon* cookies.

Chopped pine nuts

Pine nuts

PISTACHIO

*P*ISTACIA VERA, *native to central Asia, reached the Mediter-*
ranean via the Near East, brought to Rome from Syria in the
1st century. It thrives on poor rocky soil in Iran, Greece, Turkey, and
the American southwest. As the harvested nuts are dried, their shells
gape open and make the kernel easily accessible. Their natural color
is tan, but the shells are often
dyed red. The nut is
light green.

Shelled
pistachios

Pistachio
nuts

In Western cooking
these "nuts of paradise"
of the Mogul emperors
are used mostly to
decorate, but in the
Middle East they are
important ingredients.
Whole nuts provide
color, taste, and texture
in many sweetmeats and
stuffings. Pistachio ice
cream well deserves its
fame, as do salted
cocktail pistachios.

PECAN

*T*HE Carya illinoensis *produces the pecan, best of the many edible hickory nuts, the native American answer to the walnut. They are usually sold in the shell (which is thin and easy to crack) because their high oil content of 70 percent makes them go rancid quickly. Pecans are cultivated in the United States, below latitude 40° north, where the cotton and corn belts provide the best climate for them.*

A dessert nut, plain or salted, the pecan is equally good in baking or confectionery, notably pecan pie and brownies.

Shelled pecans

Pecans

MACADAMIA &
CANDLENUT

*T*HE MACADAMIA NUT (Macadamia ternifolia), *also known as Queensland nut from its origin in the forests of the northeastern Australian coast, is cultivated and exported on a large scale only on Hawaii.*

Macadamia nuts

Macadamias are among the nuts with a high oil content, prone to going rancid quickly. They are exported in vacuum packs to be eaten raw, roasted for dessert, or salted as a cocktail snack. Few are used in confectionery.

The tropical candlenuts, or kemiris, from *Aleurites moluccana*, are purgative when raw but safe once cooked. The shell is hard to crack, so the nuts are often broken. They are an essential ingredient in Indonesian and Malay cooking for thickening soups and giving flavor to *sambals*.

Candlenuts

Recipes

*All the recipes will serve 4,
but some (such as snacks and pastries)
will serve more*

SALTED ALMONDS

*½ egg white
1 lb/500 g unblanched almonds
4 teaspoons coarse sea salt*

Beat the egg white until it starts to froth. Put the nuts in a large bowl, pour over the egg white and turn the nuts in it with your hands to coat them evenly. Oil two baking sheets, spread the nuts on them and sprinkle with the salt, turning the nuts to coat them. Bake in a preheated oven, 250°F, 120°C, for 30 minutes. Shake the trays a few times to stop the nuts sticking. Turn off the heat and leave the nuts in the cooling oven for 30 minutes longer. When they are completely cool, store them in an airtight container.

Glazed Walnuts

8 oz/250 g walnuts
½ cup/125 g sugar
½ cup/125 ml water
1 tablespoon oil
pepper (optional)

Put the nuts in a bowl, cover with boiling water, and leave to stand for 30 minutes to remove any bitterness. Meanwhile make a syrup with the sugar and water. Drain the nuts and stir them into the syrup. Bring back to the boil and simmer for 3 minutes, then remove the pan from the heat and leave the nuts to absorb the syrup for 3–4 hours.

Heat the oil in a large frying pan or wok. Drain the nuts thoroughly, grind black pepper over them if you wish, and add them to the pan. Toss to coat them well with the oil and fry over medium heat, turning and stirring all the time or they will stick together. Cook for 3–4 minutes, then remove the nuts from the pan, separate any that stick together, and leave to cool. Serve cold with drinks.

Variation

Glazed cashews can be prepared in the same way, but it is not necessary to blanch the nuts first.

Peanut and Cucumber Salad

A simple spicy salad based on an
Indian recipe.

1 cucumber
1 small green pepper
2 oz/50 g roasted peanuts, ground
coarsely
1 tablespoon fresh grated coconut
(optional)
2 tablespoons chopped mint
juice of 1/2 lemon
1 teaspoon sugar
salt
2 tablespoons oil
1/2 teaspoon black mustard seeds
1/2 teaspoon cumin seeds
a pinch of cayenne

Peel and seed the cucumber and dice it. Remove the seeds from the pepper and dice. Put the vegetables, nuts, and mint in a serving bowl. Stir the lemon juice and sugar together, add salt to taste and pour over. Mix well. Heat the oil in a frying pan, add the mustard seeds and when they start to pop, add the cumin and cayenne. Stir well, and when the spices darken, pour the mixture over the salad. Toss and serve.

Olive, Pomegranate, and Walnut Salad

This salad is a specialty of Gaziantep in
southeastern Turkey, a town
surrounded by groves of olive,
pomegranate, and nut trees.

2 large pomegranates
4 oz/125 g green olives, pitted and
chopped
a bunch of coriander, chopped
6–8 scallions, chopped
4 oz/125 g walnuts, chopped coarsely
3 tablespoons olive oil
1 1/2 tablespoons lemon juice
red pepper
salt

Cut open the pomegranates and extract the seeds. Combine with the olives, coriander, scallions, and walnuts. Make a piquant dressing with the remaining ingredients, toss the salad, and serve. A few shredded young sorrel leaves make a pleasant addition.

PUMPKIN AND CHESTNUT SOUFFLÉ

1 lb/500 g pumpkin purée
(see below)
3 tablespoons/50 g butter
¹/₄ teaspoon ground cinnamon
¹/₄ teaspoon ground ginger
salt and pepper
8 oz/250 g dried chestnuts,
soaked overnight
3 egg yolks
4 egg whites

To make pumpkin purée, cut a small pumpkin in half, remove the seeds and fibers, brush the flesh with a little melted butter or oil, and bake in a preheated oven, 400°F, 200°C, for 15–20 minutes. Scoop out the flesh and purée it with the butter, spices, salt, and pepper.

Boil the chestnuts in fresh water until tender – 45–60 minutes, depending on how old they are. Drain and then remove any bits of tough inner skin from the nuts, and chop or grind quite finely. Stir into the pumpkin purée. Separate the eggs; stir the yolks into the vegetable purée. Whisk the whites until they form peaks, and fold them in as lightly as possible. Pour the mixture into a buttered 1-quart/1.2-liter soufflé dish and bake in a preheated oven, 400°F, 200°C, for 20 minutes, when the soufflé should be well risen and just set in the middle.

TROPICAL CRAB SALAD

12 oz/375 g white crabmeat
1 papaya
1/2 small melon
1 avocado
salad leaves
3 oz/75 g macadamia nuts, chopped
5 tablespoons sunflower oil
2 tablespoons lemon juice
1 teaspoon grated lemon zest
1/4 teaspoon dry mustard
salt and pepper

Flake the crabmeat. Cut the papaya, melon, and avocado into cubes. Arrange the salad leaves on plates or in a bowl, put the crab and fruit on top. Scatter the nuts over the salad. Make a dressing with the remaining ingredients, spoon it over the salad and serve.

LEEKS WITH GARLIC AND BRAZIL NUTS

1 lb/500 g leeks, sliced
1 1/2 tablespoons/25 g butter
2 garlic cloves, crushed
1 tablespoon lemon juice
2 teaspoons Kashmiri or other curry paste
3 oz/75 g Brazil nuts, grated coarsely

Cook the leeks in the butter in a heavy pan for 10 minutes, then add the other ingredients. Cover, cook for a further 5–10 minutes, and serve. The leeks go well with lamb and with potatoes baked in their jackets.

BARLEY WITH CASHEWS AND BRUSSELS SPROUTS

3 tablespoons/50 g butter
2 onions, sliced
8 oz/250 g pearl barley
3 cups/750 ml stock
4 oz/125 g cashews, chopped
salt and pepper
8 oz/250 g small brussels sprouts

Melt half the butter in a casserole and stew the onions until soft. Stir in the barley and cook for a few minutes to coat it well with butter. Heat the stock and add it together with the cashews. Season, cover the casserole tightly and put it into a preheated oven, 350°F, 180°C, for about 45 minutes, until the barley is almost cooked and most of the liquid is absorbed.

Cook the brussels sprouts in boiling water until almost soft, then drain them and toss in the remaining butter. Stir them into the barley and cashews, and return the casserole to the oven for a further 20–30 minutes.

SPINACH WITH PINE NUTS AND RAISINS

1¹/2 lb/750 g spinach
3 tablespoons raisins
2 tablespoons olive oil
3 tablespoons/50 g butter
2 garlic cloves, chopped
3 tablespoons pine nuts
salt, pepper, and nutmeg

Wash the spinach and remove any large stalks. Drain and put it into a pan with the water that clings to it and cook, turning occasionally, until it has cooked down. Put the raisins to soak in warm water for a few minutes. Drain the spinach, squeeze out all the excess water, and cut it into strips.

Heat the oil and butter in a large pan and fry the garlic until golden, then add the spinach, drained raisins, and pine nuts. Season and cook for 5 minutes.

Dendeng

Dendeng is an Indonesian dish
of spiced beef cooked in a little
liquid until it is absorbed and the
texture of the meat becomes soft
but dry.

12 oz/375 g lean beef
6 candlenuts
10 shallots, chopped
3 garlic cloves, chopped
1 teaspoon ground galangal
1 teaspoon coriander
1/2 teaspoon cumin
4 tablespoons dry shredded coconut
2 tablespoons oil
1 piece lemon grass, bruised
grated rind of 1 lemon
salt
4–6 tablespoons water

Cut the meat into very thin,
small strips. Roast the
candlenuts in a dry frying pan
for a few minutes, then blend
them with the shallots, garlic,
and spices. Mix with the
coconut and coat the meat
thoroughly. Heat the oil and fry
the meat mixture until golden
brown. Add the lemon grass,
lemon rind, and salt to taste, and
the water. Cook very slowly for
about an hour until the meat is
soft and quite dry. Check from time to time that it is not sticking
and, if necessary, add a little
more water.

INDIAN GREEN BEANS
WITH COCONUT

1 lb/500 g green beans
2 oz/50 g fresh grated coconut
3 tablespoons chopped parsley
1 green chili, seeded and chopped
2 tablespoons dry roasted
sesame seeds
salt
1/4 teaspoon turmeric
2 tablespoons oil
1 tablespoon black mustard seeds

Cut the ends off the beans and cut them into short pieces. Mix well together the coconut, parsley, chili, and sesame seeds, and put the mixture aside. Cook the beans until almost tender in salted boiling water flavored with the turmeric. Heat the oil in a frying pan, put in the mustard seeds and when they start to pop, put in the drained beans. Cook for 2–3 minutes, then stir in the coconut mixture, remove from the heat, and serve.

LIVER SAUTÉED
WITH SHERRY AND HAZELNUTS

1 onion, sliced
2 garlic cloves, sliced
olive oil
1 lb/500 g calf's liver
flour
a small glass of dry sherry
salt and pepper
a handful of toasted hazelnuts,
chopped
a handful of parsley, chopped

Heat a little olive oil and sauté the onion and garlic until golden. Remove them from the pan. Cut the liver into thin slices, coat it in flour, and fry quickly on both sides, adding a little more oil to the pan if necessary. Return the onion and garlic to the pan, add the sherry, and season with salt and pepper. Stir in the nuts and parsley, cook for a further 2 minutes, and serve.

CHICKEN WITH CASHEWS

2 tablespoons dry sherry
1 tablespoon cornmeal
1 egg white
salt
1 lb/500 g chicken breast, cubed
2 tablespoons hoisin sauce
1 tablespoon soy sauce
2 teaspoons sesame oil
2 tablespoons oil
2 red peppers, seeded and cut in cubes
4 oz/125 g mushrooms, quartered
1 garlic clove, chopped
a small piece of fresh ginger, chopped
4 scallions, sliced thinly
3 oz/75 g roasted cashews

Mix together 1 tablespoon of sherry with the cornmeal, egg white, and a little salt, and marinate the chicken for up to 2 hours. Combine the hoisin and soy sauces with the sesame oil and put the mixture aside. Heat a wok and put in the oil. When the oil is very hot, lower the heat and stir-fry the red peppers for 1 minute. Add the mushrooms, garlic, ginger, and scallions and fry for 30 seconds, then add the chicken. Raise the heat and toss well to cook the chicken. Pour in the sauce and cook for a further minute or so until the chicken is cooked through and coated with the sauce. Stir in the nuts for the last 30 seconds, and serve.

CHICKEN BRAISED IN WHITE WINE

1 chicken, cut in serving pieces
salt and pepper
flour
3 tablespoons olive oil
4 shallots, chopped
2 sprigs thyme
1 sprig marjoram
1 bay leaf
4 allspice berries
3 oz/75 g slivered almonds
4 new potatoes, peeled and quartered
a glass of dry white wine

Rub the chicken pieces with salt, pepper, and flour, and sauté them in the oil until golden brown. Add all the other ingredients, cover the pan tightly, and simmer over the lowest possible heat for about an hour, until the chicken is tender.

Variation

Use pine nuts instead of almonds.

Fesenjan

A rich Iranian dish of duck cooked in a walnut and pomegranate sauce. Chicken or pheasant can be used instead, if you wish.

1 duck, quartered
3 tablespoons/50 g butter
2 onions, sliced
10 oz/300 g walnuts, ground
2¹/₂ cups/600 ml water
salt and pepper
4 tablespoons pomegranate syrup
2 tablespoons sugar
2 tablespoons lemon juice
5 tablespoons/75 ml water

Remove all excess fat from the duck and brown it lightly in the hot butter in a large casserole.

Lift out the pieces and fry the onions until browned, then add the walnuts and 2¹/₂ cups/600 ml water, and season with salt and pepper. Return the duck to the pan, bring the sauce to the boil, then cover and simmer for about 1 hour, until the duck is almost tender.

Stir the pomegranate syrup and sugar into the lemon juice and water. Skim as much fat as possible from the top of the sauce, then stir in the pomegranate mixture. If the sauce is too thick, add a little more water. Simmer for another 30 minutes until the sauce is quite dark. Serve with rice.

INDONESIAN
PEANUT SAUCE

This sauce is excellent with satay (see below), rice, or vegetables.

1 tablespoon peanut oil
1 lb/500 g onions, chopped finely
1 garlic clove, chopped
1 teaspoon ground cumin
1/2 teaspoon ground ginger
3/4 cup/175 g peanut butter
2 tablespoons coconut cream
chili powder
salt

Heat the oil in a heavy pan and add the onions, garlic, cumin, and ginger. Stir well, turn the heat down very low, and add the peanut butter and coconut cream. Cover and leave to cook for 2–3 hours. Stir occasionally to make sure it doesn't stick, and if necessary add a little water. Eventually the sauce will become thick and smooth when stirred – you can put it through a food processor if you wish, but with long slow cooking this should not be necessary. Stir in chili powder and salt to taste, cook for a further 10–15 minutes, and serve.

PORK SATAY

1 1/2 lb/750 g pork loin
a small piece of ginger, crushed
2 garlic cloves, crushed
1 teaspoon ground coriander
1 tablespoon peanut oil
1 tablespoon/15 g coconut cream
soaked in 5 tablespoons water

Cut the pork into small cubes. Combine all the other ingredients in a blender to make a smooth marinade. Let the pork marinate for at least 2 hours, then thread the pieces onto small wooden skewers and grill for 5–6 minutes, turning as necessary. Serve with Indonesian peanut sauce.

ROMESCO SAUCE

This versatile Spanish sauce accompanies fish or shellfish, boiled vegetables and vegetable salads. In Spain it is made with the aromatic romesco pepper, but you can use a sweet red pepper and a pinch of cayenne instead.

1 dried romesco pepper or 1 sweet red
pepper and a pinch of cayenne
4 garlic cloves, unpeeled
3 medium tomatoes
10 hazelnuts
10 almonds
1 tablespoon chopped parsley
2 tablespoons wine vinegar
5 tablespoons/75 ml olive oil
salt and pepper

Remove the seeds from the romesco pepper and soak the pepper in water for 30 minutes. If using a fresh red pepper place this, with the garlic, tomatoes, and nuts, on a baking tray and put into a preheated oven, 400°F, 200°C. Remove the nuts after a few minutes when lightly toasted, the garlic and tomatoes when soft, and the pepper when the skin has blistered – it will take about 25 minutes. Peel all the vegetables; if you used a romesco pepper, drain it. Pound or process the nuts, garlic, and pepper (and cayenne if using). Add the tomatoes and parsley and blend well. Beat in the vinegar and oil as if making mayonnaise, and add salt and pepper (and a little more cayenne if you wish). Leave at room temperature for at least 2 hours before serving.

RICE PUDDING
WITH SAFFRON AND NUTS

This is very different from
Western rice pudding; it has the
consistency of a thick,
rich cream.

1/3 cup/75 g long-grain rice
5 cups/1.2 liters milk
1/2 cup/125 g sugar
bruised seeds of 6 cardamoms
2 oz/50 g dried apricots, chopped
1/2 teaspoon saffron threads
1 tablespoon rose water
2 oz/50 g blanched almonds, chopped
2 oz/50 g pistachios, chopped

Wash the rice, bring the milk to
the boil, and stir in the rice. Cook
over high heat for 1 minute, then
turn the heat down very low and
cook for a further 10 minutes,
stirring all the time. Leave to
cook slowly for 1 1/2 hours,
stirring occasionally.
Add the sugar, cardamom, and
apricots and cook for a further
30 minutes, until the pudding
thickens. Soak the saffron
threads in the rose water for
20–30 minutes and stir them in
with most of the nuts. Simmer
for another 5 minutes, then pour
the pudding into a shallow bowl.
Sprinkle the remaining nuts
over the top, and chill
before serving.

DATE AND
WALNUT DESSERT

This dessert has its origins in the
southern republics of the USSR,
the region of the Caucasus
mountains.

8 oz/250 g dates, chopped and pitted
4 oz/125 g walnuts, chopped
1/2 teaspoon ground cinnamon
2–3 tablespoons brandy

Put all the ingredients into a
food processor or pound in a
mortar until you have a fairly
smooth texture. Spread the
paste about 1/2 in/1 cm thick on a
lightly oiled tray, cut into
squares, and chill briefly.
Excellent served with coffee.

APRICOT AND PISTACHIO DESSERT

8 oz/250 g semidried apricots,
chopped
4 oz/125 g shelled fresh pistachios,
chopped
2–3 tablespoons rum

Put the apricots, pistachios, and rum into the food processor or pound in a mortar to a rough purée. Spread to dry and cool as for *Date and Walnut Dessert,* opposite below, and serve cut in squares.

PISTACHIO SHORTBREAD

3 oz/75 g shelled pistachios
1/4 cup/50 g vanilla sugar°
1 1/8 cups/150 g flour
1/4 teaspoon baking powder
salt
1/2 cup/125 g butter

Heat the oven to 400°F, 200°C. Put the pistachios on a baking tray and toast them until they are just turning brown, about 6–8 minutes. Remove from the oven and leave to cool, then grind them finely with the vanilla sugar. Turn the oven down to 325°F, 160°C.
Sift together the flour, baking powder, and a pinch of salt. Add the nut and sugar mixture and rub in the butter, gradually

working the mixture to a stiff dough. Roll out on a floured surface to about 1/2 in/1 cm thick and cut into fingers or rounds. Put the shortbread on baking sheets and bake for 35–40 minutes, or until lightly colored.

Variation
Replace the ground pistachios with ground almonds and mix with the sugar before adding to the flour.

°Vanilla sugar is made by keeping a vanilla bean in a jar of sugar, and replenishing the sugar as you use it.

PECAN PIE

1 1/8 cups/150 g flour
salt
5 tablespoons/75 g butter
1 egg yolk
2 tablespoons water
2 eggs
1 cup/175 g soft brown sugar
1 tablespoon flour
4 tablespoons milk
4 tablespoons melted butter
8 oz/250 g pecans, broken in pieces
2/3 cup/150 ml whipping cream
1 tablespoon powdered sugar
1 tablespoon bourbon whisky

Make the pastry: add a pinch of salt to the flour, cut the butter into small pieces and rub it into the flour until it resembles coarse crumbs. Whisk the egg yolk with the water and blend into the flour mixture until it is smooth and forms a ball. Leave to rest for 5 minutes, then press with the hands to line a 9-in/23-cm tart pan. It is easier to pat the pastry over the bottom and sides of the pan than to roll it first, but make sure it is even and not too thick.

Beat the eggs lightly and whisk in the sugar, flour, milk, and butter until smooth. Stir in the pecans and pour the filling into the pastry shell. Bake in a preheated oven, 425°F, 220°C, for 10 minutes, then lower the heat to 350°F, 180°C, and bake for a further 35–40 minutes. Serve warm or cold with whipped cream flavored with the sugar and bourbon.

CHESTNUT DESSERT

1¹/₂ lb/750 g chestnuts
2 cloves
1 cup/250 g sugar
3 eggs
a few marrons glacés

Boil the chestnuts with the cloves, then peel and purée them in a vegetable mill. (If you prefer to omit this step you can use canned chestnut purée, with a little powdered clove added, but the taste will not be quite as good.) Beat together the sugar and egg yolks until pale and creamy, then stir in the chestnut purée. Beat the whites till they stand in peaks and fold them into the mixture.

Butter an ovenproof dish, such as a soufflé dish, and pour in the mixture. Cook in a preheated oven, 300°F, 150°C, for 45 minutes. When the dessert is cold, sprinkle the top with small pieces of marrons glacés and serve with cream.

ITALIAN CHESTNUT CAKE

This flat cake, made with chestnut flour, is a specialty of Florence. Chestnut flour can be bought from Italian shops and delicatessens.

3 tablespoons sultana raisins
1³/₄ cups/250 g chestnut flour
salt
3 tablespoons olive oil
3 tablespoons pine nuts
a sprig of rosemary

Soak the sultanas in warm water. Add a pinch of salt to the flour and 2 tablespoons of the oil, then a little at a time, add enough water (about 2 cups/450 ml) to make a soft dough. Beat well and turn into an oiled shallow cake pan (9 in/23 cm in diameter). Drain the sultanas and scatter them over the top with the pine nuts and rosemary leaves. Sprinkle with the remaining oil and bake in a preheated oven, 325°F, 190°C, for about 50 minutes, or until the top is covered with a network of cracks. Cool in the pan on a rack.

INDEX

ACKNOWLEDGMENTS

The publishers would like to thank the following:

JACKET
· PHOTOGRAPHY ·
DAVE KING

· TYPESETTING ·
TRADESPOOLS LTD
FROME

· ILLUSTRATOR ·
JANE THOMSON

PHOTOGRAPHIC
· ASSISTANCE ·
JONATHAN BUCKLEY

· REPRODUCTION ·
COLOURSCAN
SINGAPORE

PAGE 5 RETROGRAPH ARCHIVE COLLECTION, LONDON

GWEN EDMONDS FOR ADDITIONAL HELP
KARL SHONE FOR PHOTOGRAPHY ON PAGES 6-7, 12-13

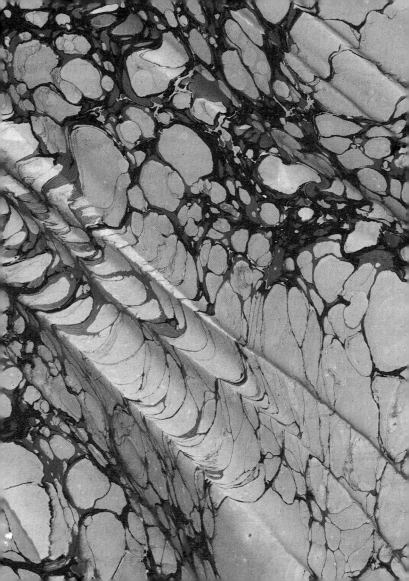